Adding up

Dorothy Einon

Illustrated by Sue Cony   Story by Claire Llewellyn

Jazz   Chip

MARSHALL PUBLISHING•LONDON

Jazz and Chip are getting ready to clean the house.

Jazz has 2 brushes and Chip has 1.

How many brushes do they have altogether?

Jazz and Chip are tidying the hall. Chip has picked up 3 shoes. Jazz has picked up 1 shoe.

How many shoes have they picked up altogether?

Jazz and Chip are tidying their toys. Jazz is holding 4 toys. Chip has 4 toys too.

How many toys are they holding altogether?

How many toys have they put on the shelves?

Find out here!

Jazz and Chip are putting away their clothes. Jazz has 4 T-shirts. Chip has 3 T-shirts.

Jazz and Chip have finished tidying up. They are having a snack in the garden. Jazz has 5 biscuits. Chip has 5 biscuits too.

How many biscuits do they have altogether?

 add makes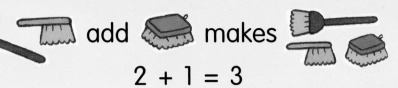

2 + 1 = 3

 add makes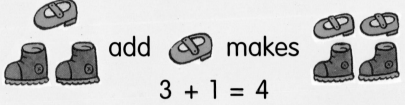

3 + 1 = 4

 add makes

4 + 4 = 8

 add makes

4 + 3 = 7

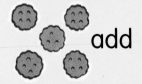 add 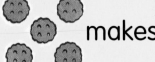 makes

5 + 5 = 10

Guide to

All Saints Nort   York

Andrew A. Horsman

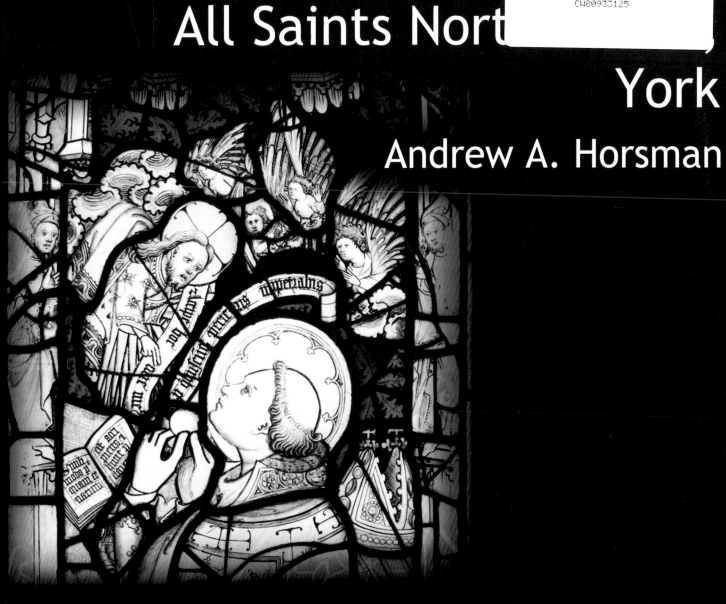

All Saints Church North Street, York YO1 6JD
www.allsaints-northstreet.org.uk
ISBN *9780954553159*

All Saints exists for the glory of God, and a place of Christian worship has stood on this historic site for at least 1100 years. Situated in the shadow of York Minster, in the bustling heart of the city, the church is a sanctuary of prayerful peace, where the sacraments of the Christian faith are celebrated, and the mission of the Church is lived out. In our worship, we reflect the historic offering of the Church, centring our liturgy on the Mass, and the commandment of Jesus Christ himself, to "do this in memory of me." (Luke 22:19)

Our church is a Grade I listed building, and notable for containing the finest collection of medieval glass in York – after the Minster, of course – including the famous "Pricke of Conscience" window. Over the years, several restorations have been undertaken, including the 2022-23 restoration of the windows, and the 2012 restoration of the shrine of Our Lady of North Street, with its beautiful statue of the Blessed Virgin Mary. The chancel screen is early 20th century, as is the anchorite's house, and the organ dates from 1996 and incorporates parts from the earlier instrument of 1867. You can read more about the art and architecture of the church in this guidebook, and during your visit we hope you will encounter both the beauty of its history and the living tradition for which it exists today.

Whether worshipper, pilgrim, resident, or visitor, you are very welcome in this place – to light a candle and say a prayer, to find peace and stillness in the humdrum of daily life, or to experience the beauty of this hallowed place, as so many others have done before. May you see a glimpse of heaven here and encounter the living God, whom this church exists to proclaim and glorify.

The QR codes
These codes appear on most pages of this Guidebook. When scanned they open a page on the church website containing further information on that topic.
This extra information will be updated to reflect ongoing research. Don't forget to check it every now and then.

⟳) The Lady Chapel

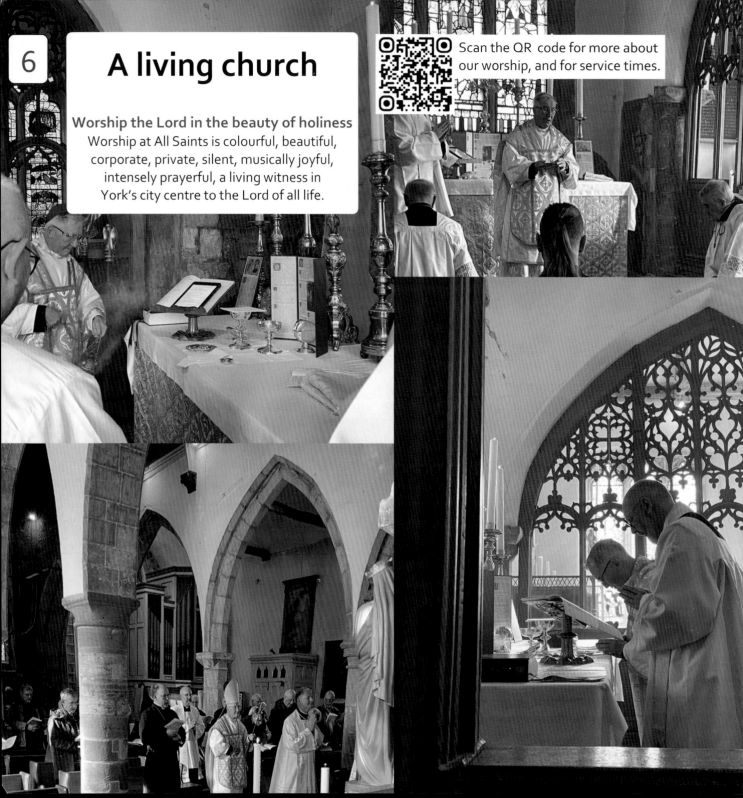

6

A living church

Scan the QR code for more about our worship, and for service times.

Worship the Lord in the beauty of holiness
Worship at All Saints is colourful, beautiful,
corporate, private, silent, musically joyful,
intensely prayerful, a living witness in
York's city centre to the Lord of all life.

The Stained-Glass Windows of All Saints

All Saints North Street is unique even among York's wealth of surviving medieval parish churches. More of its structure, fittings and decorations have survived than in any other York church. Above all, the stained glass windows are the chief glory of All Saints.

Why are the windows in All Saints important?
The ten that survive from the years from 1330 to about 1440 form one of the great set pieces of English medieval art. They contain more good medieval glass than almost any other parish church in England.

Why are these windows unique?
Many of the subjects they depict are highly unusual and even unique among medieval windows: everyday domestic scenes are shown; there are disabled people in several windows; there is text in English; they include the only 'indulgence' in glass in England and the only illustrated version of one poem in Europe.

Why did medieval churches have stained-glass windows?
Medieval people loved bright colours and filled their churches with them, painting the walls and colouring the window glass. Churches became joyfully vibrant spaces, enriching people's often drab lives, testifying to the colour and beauty of God's creation.

The windows told stories of biblical and religious truths for an age when almost nobody could possess expensively hand-copied Bibles or other books. They presented these truths pictorially, accessible to people who couldn't read. They summoned Christians to repentance and renewal by reminding them that the Christian life is lived surrounded by the saints. They gave a foretaste of heaven.

Why does so little medieval glass survive?
Glass breaks easily, both accidentally and deliberately. The religious upheavals of the 16th century (the Reformation) and the 17th century (the English Civil War) led to widespread destruction.

Disasters in the past

The windows have survived other disasters besides deliberate destruction. At some time between 1730 and 1846 an unknown catastrophe wrecked many of the windows. Some were totally lost, and some others fell out and were put back wrongly, becoming unrecognizably jumbled up.

This could have been because of a huge storm like the one that struck the north of England in October 1756, felling trees, blowing down buildings and sinking ships.

Stained-glass windows that have fallen out are like a jigsaw puzzle of many pieces but with no picture on the lid of the box. After atrocious weather the priority will be to put the pieces back anyhow so as to make the building watertight. Re-forming the original pictures would be a lower priority.

Today there are still window panels in All Saints like

this one, *above*, consisting of jumbled fragments and we have no idea where they originally went. And the windows on pages 30 and 32 were restored to something like their original shape only in the 1960s.

(left) This orphan panel has lost the rest of its glass.

(below) Two musicians serenading our Lady (p. 32).

10 The St Thomas window

This window dates from around 1420 and stands beside the altar of St Thomas the Martyr. This is Thomas Becket, the archbishop of Canterbury who was murdered in his cathedral in 1170 on the orders of king Henry II. The window also features his biblical namesake, St Thomas the Apostle.

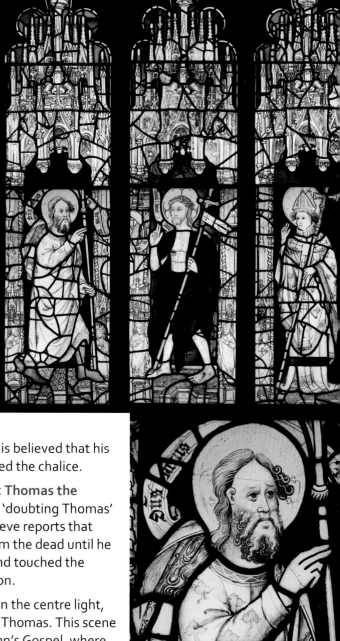

St Thomas the Martyr, victim of Henry II's fury

We would expect an image of Becket in this window, and indeed in the right-hand light is an archbishop, identified by the linen pallium around his neck. But all is not as it seems.

Wherever you see a QR code, scan it for more information.

Another king Henry's fury

In 1534 Henry VIII declared himself head of the Church of England. He was deeply embarrassed by the widespread popularity of St Thomas, the murdered archbishop who had stood up for the Church against his king's tyranny. In 1538 Henry VIII ordered all images of Becket to be destroyed.

Windows were of course an easy target, and it is highly likely that the image in this window of St Thomas the Martyr was smashed then.

The archbishop in the right-hand light of the window is in fact **St William of York**, moved here in the 1970s, the only survivor of an otherwise unknown window. William was also murdered in his cathedral, York Minster, but a few years before Becket, in 1154. He was

saying Mass, and it is believed that his archdeacon poisoned the chalice.

In the left light is **St Thomas the Apostle** (*right*), the 'doubting Thomas' who refused to believe reports that Christ had risen from the dead until he had himself seen and touched the wounds of crucifixion.

The risen Christ is in the centre light, showing himself to Thomas. This scene is taken from St John's Gospel, where Thomas responds 'My Lord and my God'. This confession of faith appears in Latin on the scroll behind Thomas's head.

(right) St William of York, archbishop of York from 1141 to 1147 and again from 1153 to his murder in 1154.

The two spells were separated by a period of exile, as his appointment to York became the subject of political power-games involving king Stephen, a civil war, various religious orders, and the deaths of two popes.

He was very popular in York, and his return in summer 1154 was welcomed by such large crowds that the Ouse Bridge in York collapsed under their weight. Miraculously no-one drowned. Only a month later William was murdered.

(above) The risen Christ shows Thomas the wounds in his hands, feet and chest.

The complicated Latin scroll beside his head reads 'Thomas, reach hither thy hand and thrust it into my side. Blessed are they that have not seen and yet have believed', John 20.27-29.

(right) The window to the west of the St Thomas window contains a miscellany of coats of arms from various sources and centuries. This panel has the arms of England and France quartered. In the lower right quarter is a striking example of medieval craftsmanship: the golden fleur-de-lys on the far right is actually inserted into a hole cut in the blue background glass. The modern glazier who made the upper left quarter didn't dare do that.

The Corporal Acts of Mercy window (c. 1420)

The important parts of this wonderful window are the six panels in the centre, two in each of the three lights, beneath the elaborate canopies and above the kneeling donors.

They illutrate the six acts of mercy towards the needy commended by Jesus in the parable of the sheep and the goats (Matthew 25). They are:

Feeding the hungry, giving drink to the thirsty, welcoming strangers, clothing the naked, visiting the sick, bringing relief to prisoners.

Theology by numbers

Medieval piety called them the 'Corporal Acts of Mercy', and added a seventh, Burying the dead. Thus there were said to be seven Corporal Acts of Mercy, as there were four Cardinal Virtues, three Theological Virtues, seven Deadly Sins, and seven Spiritual Acts of Mercy.

The details of this window (see opposite page) contain fascinating insights into daily life in 1410. Many of these are rarely seen in stained glass, such as disabled people, beggars, a blind man, prisoners, and a domestic interior.

The Blackburn family

The window was given as a memorial to Nicholas Blackburn, father and grandfather of the Blackburns shown at the foot of the great East Window (p. 22). Hence the window itself is the seventh 'Corporal Act', Burying the dead. The Blackburns were a family of rich merchant traders living and working in North Street. All Saints was their parish church.

The bottom panels, two of them containing kneeling figures, were not originally part of this window. The one on the left is probably Reginald Bawtrie, from a lost window for which in 1429 he bequeathed the enormous sum of 100 shillings (over ten thousand pounds in today's money). He is singing from the Litany of Saints, and his book is open at St Cecilia (his wife's name), the patron saint of music and musicians.

(left light upper) **Feeding the hungry**. A good man stands at the door of his house, as his servant (wearing the same livery as his master) gives loaves of bread from a large basket to the hungry. The one at the front is lame and leans on a crutch.

The 'good man' is clearly recognisable in all six panels of this window, with his forked beard and distinctive cap. He is likely to be merely a stylized figure, not intended to be a realistic portrait of Nicholas Blackburn.

(centre light upper) **Giving drink to the thirsty**. The crippled beggar in the foreground has leather knee pads and little three-legged hand-stools. It is rare to see a disabled person depicted in a window like this. The servant on the right is ready with extra pitchers of water and empty drinking bowls.

(right light upper) **Giving hospitality to strangers**. These particular strangers seem to be pilgrims, en route to a distant holy place. Each carries a pilgrim's staff. The man in the red cloak is blind—he is being led on a rein.

(left light lower) **Clothing the naked**. The good man is handing a warm red cloak to a man dressed only in a thin undershirt, who might otherwise die of the cold.

(right light lower) **Bringing relief to prisoners**. The good man is giving them food. The unfortunate prisoners are manacled with neck-, wrist- and leg-irons, and have their feet in the stocks.

(centre light lower) **Visiting the sick**. A man is lying sick in bed as his wife looks anxiously on. Sickness meant no income and the threat of poverty, so the good man places a gift of coins on the bedspread. The bedspread is beautifully embroidered, and the same fabric covers the headboard of the bed. It is very rare to see such a depiction of domestic furnishings in a medieval window. The bedspread reappears in the adjacent Pricke of Conscience window, 'Day' 14 (p. 17).

The chair in the sickroom foreground looks like a commode but is in fact a normal chair of the period. When commodes were invented they were camouflaged as chairs, and when the fashion in chair design moved on, commodes were left behind!

14 The Pricke of Conscience window (c. 1420)

This, the finest window in All Saints, is unique in Europe for illustrating this popular poem scene-by-scene with the lines of the poem beneath each scene. It is also one of very few medieval windows in England to have writing in English not Latin.

'The Pricke of Conscience', a medieval poem
'The Pricke of Conscience' is a long devotional poem which was very popular in its day. It was written around 1340, we don't know by whom, in the Northumbrian dialect of Middle English.

Most devotional works were written in Latin, but near the end the anonymous poet tells us why he has written *in English*: it is because dim-witted English people will not take the trouble to learn any other language!

To *pricke* is to stimulate or goad into action. The poem seeks to goad the reader's conscience into meditating on the fragility of human life and the need for salvation.

'Northumbria' was the eastern part of England from the river Humber north to the Scottish border.

'Middle English' was the form of the English language spoken from about 1150 to about 1500. The Middle English letter þ ('thorn') starts off each Day's inscription. Its sound is 'th', though it is often mistaken for 'y', as in 'ye olde'.

The end of the world
Mid-way through the poem comes a section about the apocalyptic events expected to be experienced at the end of the world. Medieval piety went through periods of intense apocalyptic expectation, generally associated with the approach of significant dates like AD 1000 or 1500. This fits with the date of around 1410 for the window. Moreover the Black Death, which killed one third of the populations of Europe, was still within living memory (some 60 years before). Disasters were news!

The top of the window arch, left, was chopped off some 60 years after the window was made, so that the angel ceiling installed in the 1470s would fit. Evidently the earlier ceiling was higher.

15

Who paid for the window?

Across the bottom you can see the donors of the window, all piously kneeling. They were members of three Yorkshire families named Henrison, Hessle and Wiloby.

The apocalyptic events of the Last Fifteen Days

These include tsunamis, earthquakes, the sea catching fire, meteorite impact, volcanic eruptions, wildfires, global warming, pandemics and death everywhere, and finally the whole cosmos going up in flames.

The point is not the gruesomeness but the reality of the threats—threats that are eerily familiar to us in today's world too.

Get your bearings

The window is read from left to right and, unusually, **from bottom to top**.

At the bottom are the donors. Directly above them are the first 3 of the 15 panels describing the apocalyptic terrors of the last 15 'days' of the world. The next 3 are in the row above that, and so on.

The poet makes it clear that he does not claim that each 'day' is 24 hours. He says he doesn't know how long each 'day' will actually be.

Day 1

þe j day xl cubetes certayne
þe see sall ryse vp aboue ilk mountayne

The first day the sea shall rise beyond doubt
forty cubits above every mountain

On the first 'day' the sea floods the land.

Day 2

þe seconde day þe see sall be
so lawe as all men sall it cee

The second day the sea shall be
so low that men shall scarcely see it

On the second 'day' the sea recedes entirely, exposing the sea-bed.

Day 3

þe iij day yt sall be playne
and stand as yt was agayne

The third day the sea shall be level
and stand as it was again

On the third 'day' the sea, racing in from the left, regains its normal level.

These events of 'days' 1—3 strikingly recall what actually happens in a tsunami: the sea floods, then withdraws, then returns to normal. In the great Lisbon earthquake of 1755 many of those who survived the initial tsunami flood went to see the extraordinary phenomenon of the emptying of the harbour, and were promptly drowned when the sea rushed back in.

Day 4

þe ferth day fisches sal make roryng
hidus & hevy to mannes heryng

*The fourth day fishes shall make a
roaring noise
hideous and dreary to men's hearing*

On the fourth 'day' fish leap out of the
sea with a hideous roaring. The sea has
become oxygen-starved, as if from a
submarine volcanic eruption which has
filled it with methane.

Day 5

þe fift day þe sea sall bryn
and all þe waters that may ryn

*The fifth day the sea shall burn
and all the waters as they shall flow*

Continuing the 'eruption' theme, on
the fifth 'day' flames appear on the
sea as the methane ignites, giving the
appearance of the sea on fire.

Day 6

þe sext day sall herbes & trees
wyth blody dropes þat grysely bees

*The sixth day shall plants and trees
with bloody drops that are repulsive*

On the sixth 'day' grass and trees
exude drops of blood like dew, filling
people with horror and making crops
inedible, hence threatening
starvation.

Day 7

þe seuent day howses mon fall
castels & towres & ilk a wall

*The seventh day houses must fall
castles and towers and every wall*

On the seventh 'day' buildings of all
kinds are laid low—not just the flimsy
dwellings of the poor but substantial
and solid stone-built ones.

Day 8

þe viii day þe roches & stanes
sall bryn toged all at anes

*The eighth day thet rocks and stones
shall burn [strike] together all at once*

On the eighth 'day' rocks and stones
are consumed by fire—as you might
see in a terrifying volcanic eruption.

Day 9

þe ix day erthdyn sall be
generally in ilk contre

*The ninth day shall be an earthquake
generally in every country*

On the ninth 'day' the whole world is
stricken with earthquakes.

---

*Prominent among the Day 7 ruins is a fallen church spire, looking **very like the spire of All Saints,** less than 25 years old at the time
the window was made. Do we imagine the glass painter poking fun at the stonemasons? — 'Now look at the spire you're so proud of.'*

Day 10

þe tende day for neuen
erthe sal be playne & euen

*The tenth day once again
the earth shall be level and flat*

On the tenth 'day' hills and mountains
are levelled in a cataclysmic upheaval.

Day 11

þe xi day sall men com owte
of their holes & wende a bowte

*The eleventh day men shall come out
of their holes and run about*

On the eleventh 'day' people emerge
from hiding in caves and wander about
like madmen, out of their minds. (One
timidly refuses to come out!)

Day 12

þe xij day sal dede men banes
be samen sett & ryse al at anes

*The twelfth day shall dead men's bones
be set together and rise all at once*

On the twelfth 'day' the bones of the
dead are raised and the dead
reconstituted ready for the final death.

Interestingly, the poem usually has the twelfth and thirteenth 'days' in the reverse order to the window.

Day 13

þe thirtend day suthe sall
sternes & the heuen fall

*The thirteenth day in truth shall
stars fall from the Heaven*

On the thirteenth 'day' the stars and
other heavenly bodies (meteorites,
asteroids?) fall from the sky, with
devastating consequences.

Day 14

þe xiiij day all þat liues þan
sall dy bathe childe man & woman

*The fourteenth day all those that live
shall die, both child, man and woman*

On the fourteenth 'day' death stalks
the land and all die. (Note the fine
embroidered bedspread, in a very rare
depiction of an ordinary house interior.)

Day 15

þe xv day þus sal betide
þe werlde satt bryn on ilk a side

*The fifteenth day shall happen thus:
the world shall burn on every side*

On the fifteenth 'day' the whole world
goes up in flames.

The Last Judgment

Above the fifteen panels, in the 'tracery lights' can be seen the Judgment. St Peter, on the left and holding a key, welcomes the blessed at the gate of heaven. Demons, on the right, consign the damned to hell. (See illustrations on p. 19.)

Both the blessed and the damned are shown in plain white. It is St Peter and the demons who are in prominent colour.

These scenes are the logical conclusion of the fifteen 'doom' panels. At the end of the world all will face the Judgment—they bring it home to the individual viewer of the window, with a dire warning.

The chopped-off top of the window probably contained glass showing Christ in Majesty, the usual visual climax of depictions of the Last

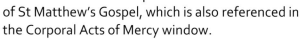

Judgment. He would be facing us, with the damned on his left and the blessed on his right. This is as in the Great Assize parable of St Matthew's Gospel, which is also referenced in the Corporal Acts of Mercy window.

The window as a whole thus forms a powerful call to recollection and sincere repentance. To fallen humans this is difficult, next to impossible. But all is not lost. Our Lady stands right next to the window—and has done ever since the window was made—signifying that she is available with her powerful intercession to pray for us to her Son, Jesus, known in the sacrament of the altar. The window, statue and altar thus form a spiritual unity of great power. They afford a fascinating glimpse into late medieval spirituality.

The poem's text

To give a flavour of this extraordinary poem, below are the lines that refer to the last fifteen 'days', lines 4758-4816 of the 9624 lines of the poem. Alongside them is a simple verse rendering in modern English.

St Peter welcomes the blessed into heaven

Demons push the damned down into hell, whose fearsome jaws gape

---

Þe **first day** of þas fifteen days,
Þe se sal ryse, als þe bukes says,
Abowen þe heght of ilka mountayne,
Fully fourty cubyttes certayne,
And in his stede even upstande,
Als an heghe hille dus on þe lande.

Þe **secunde day**, þe se sal be swa law
Þat unnethes men sal it knaw.

Þe **thred day**, þe se sal seme playn
And stand even in his cours agayn,
Als it stode first at þe bygynnyng,
With-outen mare rysyng or fallyng.

Þe **fierth day**, sal swilk a wonder be,
Þe mast wondreful fisshes of þe se
Sal com to-gyder and mak swilk roryng
Þat it sal be hydus til mans heryng.
Bot what þat roryng sal signify,
Na man may whit, bot God almyghty.

Þe **fift day**, the se sal brynne
And alle watters als þai sal rynne;
And þat sal last fra þe son rysyng
Til þe tyme of þe son doun ganging.

Þe **sext day**, sal spryng a blody dewe
On grisse and tres, als it sal shewe.

Þe **sevend day** byggyns doun sal falle
And grete castels, and tours with-alle.

Þe **eght day**, hard roches and stanes
Sal strik togyder, alle attanes.
An ilkan of þam sal other doun cast,
And ilkan agayn other hortel fast,
swa þat ilka stan, on divers wyse,
Sal sonder other in thre partyse.

On **the first day** of the fifteen days
The sea shall rise, as the book says,
About as much as a mountain's height
(That's forty cubits tall all right)
And so the sea will rise and stand
Just like a hill does on the land.

The second day the sea will fall
So low that people will see under all.

The third day, the sea will seem plain
And act as it normally does again
Just like it did first, there at the start
No more rising or falling of every part

The fourth day, there will wonder be:
The most crazy fishes of the sea
Shall come together and make such a din
Hideous to hear when they begin,
But what they mean by all their cries
No-one but God will ever surmise.

On **the fifth day**, the sea will burn
And other waters run and turn.
And this will last from the sun's rise
Until the sun sets in the skies.

On **the sixth will** form a bloody dew
On grass and tree, all plain to view.

The seventh day, strong buildings will fall,
Along with great castles, then towers tall.

The eighth day, hard stones and rock
By themselves will crash and knock.
And one shall smash the other past
Then that one bounce and hurtle fast
Then other stones, differently,
Will shatter each other in pieces three.

Þe **neghend day**, gret erthedyn sal be,
Generaly in ilka contre;
And swa gret erthdyn als sal be þan
Was never hard, sythen þe world bygan.

Þe **tend day** þar-aftir to neven,
Þe erthe sal be made playn and even,
For hills and valeis sal turned be
In-til playn, and made even to se.

Þe **ellevend day** men sal com out
Of caves, and holes and wend about,
Als wode men, þat ne witt can;
And nane sal spek til other þan.

Þe **twelfte day** aftir, þe sternes alle
And þe signes fra þe heven sal falle.

Þe **thredend day** sal dede men banes
Be sett to-gyder, and ryse al attanes,
And aboven on þair graves stand;
Þis sal byfalle in ilka land.

Þe **fourtend day**, al þat lyves þan
Sal dighe, childe, man and woman;
For þai shalle with þam rys ogayn
Þat byfor war dede, outher til ioy or payn.

Þe **fiftend day**, þos sal betyde,
Alle þe world sal bryn on ilk syde,
And þe erthe whar we now duelle,
Until the utter end of alle helle.

The ninth day there will be an earthquake
And all the country wide will shake
A bigger quake there never was than
This one now, since the world began.

The tenth day (to give it its name)
The earth shall be made flat and plain,
For hills and valleys shall turned be
Into a large plain, and made smooth to see.

The eleventh day, people will come out
Of caves and holes, and wander about
Like madmen do, who've lost their mind
And no-one will speak to the people they find.

The twelfth day after, the stars and all
The planets in the high heavens shall fall.

The thirteeth day shall dead people's bones
Be put back together, and then rise all alone
And each above their own grave stand;
And this shall happen over all the land.

The fourteenth day shall all living then
Die: children, women, men
For they will with them rise again
Who were then dead - to joy, or pain.

The fifteenth day, this shall transpire:
All the world will burn in fire -
Yes, all the earth where now we dwell -
Until the final death of Hell.

Modern English version by Dominic Horsman

The Lady Chapel East window (c. 1330)

This is the earliest window in All Saints. Its small crowded scenes and intense colours are typical of the century it was made. They contrast with the windows of the following century like the St Thomas window (p. 10), which usually focus on a few large figures and allow more light through.

The story of salvation

The six main panels tell the Christian story of salvation. They are in this order:

3 4 6

1 2 5

1 The Annunciation—the archangel Gabriel announces to the virgin Mary that she is to be the mother of God's Son
2 The Nativity—the birth of Jesus
3 The Adoration of the Magi—the three Kings offer gifts to Jesus
4 The Crucifixion—Jesus dies on the cross
5 The Resurrection of Jesus—he rises from the tomb
6 The Coronation of our Lady— Mary is crowned Queen of Heaven.

Using the latest technology

The window's painters embraced the most up-to-date glass-painting techniques of the 1330s. The technique of 'silver stain' had just been discovered. Silver compounds painted on to glass and fired in a kiln created a yellow colour on clear glass. For the first time it was possible to have several different colours painted on a single piece of glass. The painters of this window showed this off in panel 1, in the Angel Gabriel's wing and his blond hair and in the Virgin Mary's hair.

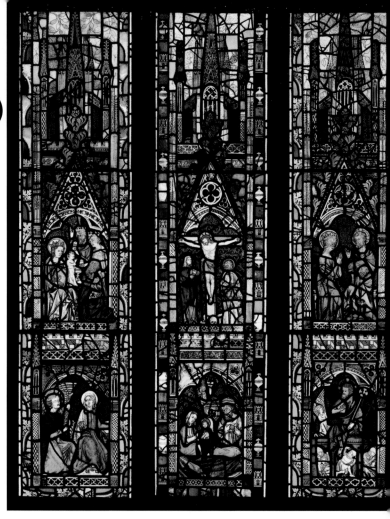

In a window this old many small pieces of glass have naturally had to be renewed down the centuries. The face of the risen Christ, bottom right (no. 5), is a clear example of a modern piece. In the panel above that (no. 6), the original faces are very pitted, probably corroded by atmospheric pollution.

This window was originally above the High Altar. The central figure of the crucified Christ would have been seen behind the Altar. A cross *on* the altar, as in modern practice, was unknown in medieval England. Each of the three east-end altars in this church has a crucifix in stained glass behind.

1 (above) The Annunciation
The angel Gabriel, left, announces to a plainly terrified Virgin Mary that she is to bear God's Son. Between the two figures is a white lily, symbolising her purity.

2 (above) The Nativity
Mary holds the Christ-child, as Joseph looks on. Joseph is shown as an older man, leaning on a stick. An ass and a friendly-looking red ox are seen above them.

3 (above) The Adoration of the Magi
The three Kings present their gifts to the (by now older) Christ-child. One of the Kings is kneeling and holds his crown. The Virgin, to emphasise her importance, is also crowned.

5 (below) The Resurrection
An angel in white removes the stone, and Jesus, alive, rises out of his tomb. The soldiers supposed to be on guard are asleep, apart from one who is bewildered and frightened.
The soldiers are wearing the very latest armour of the 1330s—the painter probably had no idea what ancient Roman armour actually looked like.

4 (below) The Crucifixion
Christ on the cross, accompanied by St Mary (on the left) and St John. According to St John's Gospel these were the only two people who remained faithful to Jesus at his cross. They are often shown flanking the cross like this.

6 (below) The Coronation of the Virgin
The glorified Christ, on the right, blesses the Virgin Mary now crowned Queen of Heaven. This was considered an important sign, showing that the redemption of humanity by Christ was complete.

22 The East window (c. 1420)

This window has been called, for its central panel, the most photogenic window in England. In that panel the Virgin Mary as a child is being taught to read and pray by her mother St Anne. It is one of the finest devotional images of our Lady to have survived from medieval England. That it is in such a fragile medium as glass makes its survival all the more remarkable.

The Blackburn family

The Blackburn family of North Street donated this window, as they did the Corporal Acts of Mercy window. As donors the Blackburns appear kneeling at the bottom with their prominent 'B' monogram—Nicholas snr is on the right with his wife Margaret, and their son Nicholas jnr on the left with *his* wife Margaret.

The Blackburns were a leading family of York merchants. They were successful traders in cloth and textiles (mercers). All Saints was the church of the mercers' guild. Nicholas snr became Lord Mayor of York in 1413, as did his son in 1429. They gave the Corporal Acts of Mercy window in memory of Nicholas snr's father.

Nicholas snr is wearing the uniform of Admiral of the Northern Fleet, a title he bought from king Henry IV—he clearly saw himself as upwardly mobile! Hedging his bets, though, he prays to God as king, in the scroll above his head.

Educated women

In an age when education for women was largely confined to the aristocracy, it is remarkable that all the women in this window are reading. With all of them—our Lady, St Anne, and both Margaret Blackburns—the words they are reading are very clearly and legibly painted in the glass for us to read too. The Blackburns may have been 'mere' merchants, but they were proud of their family's literate women.

St Anne with our Lady as a child *(right)*

In the central image of the window St Anne teaches her daughter the Virgin Mary to read and pray. It was usual for children to be taught reading by using prayers.

Fittingly the book is open at a Psalm which begins 'Hear my prayer, O Lord'. Mary is following the words with a pointer as her mother watches. In the eyes of both mother and daughter is a faraway look, as if meditating on the momentous events to come in the daughter's life.

The focus of the window is on St Anne, the main figure. The function of her daughter in the composition is to show that this is St Anne.

The Blackburns shared in the devotion to St Anne which had spread rapidly in England over the preceding century. She was seen as a vital influence on her daughter's upbringing, preparing her to become the mother of the Saviour. The Blackburn window honours her, and hence displays the Blackburn women prominently.

(left) **The Trinity in picture form** Between the kneeling Blackburns, at the foot of the centre light is a striking representation of **God the Holy Trinity**. The Father is seated on his throne, holding the crucified Son before him, and the dove of the Holy Spirit is between their two heads.

The East window
(contd.)

St John the Baptist *(this page, right)*

St John the Baptist, in the left-hand panel, is recognised by his wild hair and camel-hair robe, the rough garb of a prophet. He is shown pointing to the lamb seated on his book—in the Gospels he pointed out Christ, saying 'Behold the Lamb of God'.

The younger Blackburns *(below)*

Nicholas jnr, in the green cloak, and his wife Margaret, at prayer. She wears a white head-dress and a red robe, and is seated at a desk draped with an embroidered white cloth. He is kneeling on a cushion with gold tassels. His belt has a dagger hanging from it.

St Christopher *(this page, left)*

The right-hand panel shows Christ carried by St Christopher ('he who bears Christ'). According to legend St Christopher carried an unknown child across a river before the child revealed himself as Christ.

The scroll above Christ refers to this legend: 'Though Christopher carries me, I carry the sins of the world'.

The water has fish in it and looks as if it is flowing. It is painted on both sides of the glass to give it a 3-D effect. St Christopher's robe is hitched up to keep it dry.

The elder Blackburns *(below)*

Nicholas snr and his wife Margaret. He is resplendent in his uniform as Admiral of the Northern Fleet, with a red coat over plate armour. His helmet is beside him as he prays bareheaded. Margaret is wearing an elaborate chequered robe under a red cloak.

28 The St Nicholas Chapel
(the south chancel aisle)

This aisle was constructed in the early 14th century, and the wall between it and the Chancel was pierced with arches to give access to it. No attempt was made to copy the size and spacing of the arches on the north side of the Chancel leading to the Lady Chapel, which had been made more than a century earlier.

The east window (c. 1340)
The glass for this window was probably made shortly after that for the east window in the Lady Chapel (p. 20). It has been very heavily restored over the centuries: so many pieces have been replaced after damage that not a great deal of the original glass is left.

The central crucifix functions as the chapel's altar crucifix, exactly as in the case of the east window of the Lady Chapel, which was originally behind the High Altar.

The Leaning Window of York
Yes, the window really is this crooked! It seems that the foundations of the Chapel sank as it was being built, even before the window's stonework was finished. The glass had to be made to fit its distorted shape. The further right you go, the more pronounced the rightward lean. All three lights splay outwards towards the top.

In the upper row is, left, our Lady, unusually dressed in purple. She is medieval. In the centre is the Crucifixion. To the right is St John the Evangelist.

The placing of our Lady and St John on each side of the crucified Christ is traditional in medieval art. According to St John's gospel only these two remained faithfully by the cross when all the other disciples had fled.

In the lower row two kneeling women donors face Christ in the centre. He holds the cup of sorrow in the Garden of Gesthemane.

The St Michael and St John window
(c. 1440)
St Michael the warrior-archangel, left, faces St John the Evangelist, right. Both of them are under splendidly exuberant 'canopies'.

St Michael killing the dragon
St Michael is shown with drawn sword standing victorious on a terrible three-headed dragon.

The dragon is Satan, the old deceiver and enemy of the human race. The 'war in heaven' between the dragon and St Michael is a theme in the New Testament book of Revelation.

A tale of two St Johns
The author of the book of Revelation is known as St John the Divine (i.e. the theologian). When the window was made he was universally believed to be the same John as St John the Evangelist (i.e. the gospel-writer). This explains why St John the Evangelist appears opposite St Michael here.

Fr James Baguley, probable driving force behind most of the All Saints windows
Baguley was rector of All Saints from 1413 till his death in 1440, the period during which most of the windows were made.

Astonishingly we have a picture of him—he is shown at the extreme bottom left kneeling at a prayer desk. His tonsured head shows he is ordained.

The couple next to him are a certain Robert Chapman and his wife. Together with the unknown three on the far right they are the donors of the window.

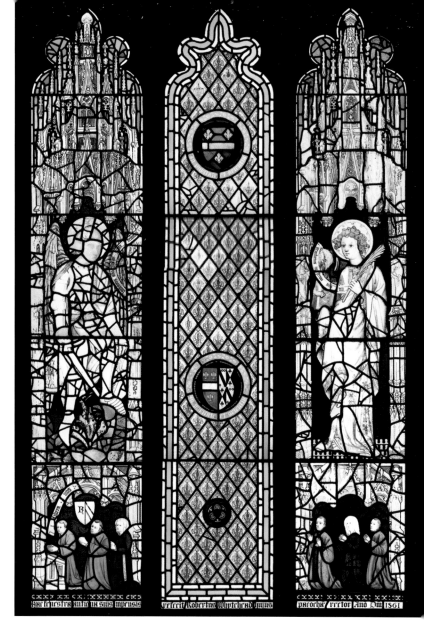

A marriage made in heaven?
In between St Michael and St John is the coat of arms of the Revd. Robert Whytehead, rector of All Saints, and his wife Henrietta Dodsworth, married here in 1858. A Latin inscription across the foot of the window says that he had this window restored at his own expense in 1861.

30 The Nine Orders of Angels window (c. 1420)

This is a story of a loss that could have been fatal but for a chance discovery.

What a mess!

Until 1965 this window looked like the illustration *below*. At some date before 1846 the glass seems to have fallen out, perhaps in a storm, and been put back randomly. Nobody knew what the window was meant to be.

Rescued by a sketch

In 1960 a 300-year-old sketch of the original window was discovered. It had been made by a man called Henry Johnston who visited the church in 1670. It showed that the window depicts 'the nine Orders of

Angels in religious belief

Angels were an important part of medieval spirituality. Ordinary people's belief in the presence of invisible beings surrounding them was a source of great strength.

This window describes angels with distinctive characters and functions. They are strong rather than bland, like the people we might think of as 'angels of mercy' who come to our aid in difficult situations.

Source: Historic England Archive

Angels' as described by Pope Gregory the Great in an influential sermon of AD 591. The window was reconstructed in 1966 using Johnston's sketch.

Above each 'Order' are fragmentary Latin words describing the function of that 'Order' according to St Gregory - see the opposite page.

Among so many faces in this window, quite a few have been lost over the centuries. But enough survive to charm us, such as the child in the 'Angels' panel, the bearded kings in 'Dominations', and the angels representing 'Thrones' and 'Powers'.

(below) The 1670 sketch that guided the 1966 restorers

(left) 'SERAPHIM, on fire with love, constantly in attendance on God.'
The seraph is entirely red, 'on fire'.
Above his head an extra pair of wings is folded, as with all the angels in the top two rows.

(left) 'CHERUBIM, knowing all things and rightly disposing them.'
Like others in the top two rows the angel has an extra pair of wings folded above his head.

(right) 'THRONES, judging all things in subjection to the judgment of God.'

(left) 'DOMINATIONS, ruling with humility, chastising with kindness.'
The angel has a sumptuously embroidered robe. Beside him are two crowned bearded kings and part of a pope.

(left) 'PRINCIPALITIES, aiding the needy, governing in the interests of the lowly.'

(right) 'POWERS, coming forth from heaven to cast down the wicked.'

(left) 'VIRTUES, working miracles and so revealing God.'

(right) 'ARCHANGELS, leading to God all that are doomed to die.'

(right) 'ANGELS, consoling the sorrowful, announcing the things of God'.
Behind the crowd is a man wearing spectacles. Could this be a self-portrait of the glass painter himself, with poor eyesight after painting these tiny pieces of glass?

The St James window (c. 1440)

This is called the St James window because it stands next to the altar of St James in the church. The three main figures in this window are the apostle St James (on the left), the Virgin and Child (centre), and St Denys the martyr-archbishop of Paris (right).

Rescued from fragments

Like the previous window (page 30) this one also had suffered serious damage and had to be reconstructed in 1966. *Below* is the chaotic 'before' image—not quite as bad as p. 30's. The three lowest panels containing circles, *right*, were blank before 1966. They now consist of miscellaneous bits and pieces of glass left over from these two recontructions.

Source: Historic England Archive

Why these three saints?

St James, our Lady and archbishop St Denys may have been favourites of whoever donated this window. But what have they in common?

A possible clue lies in the three lines of fragments of writing at the bottom right, directly above the large circle at the foot of the window containing the archbishop. These are an 'indulgence' (see opposite page), and they might just explain it.

St James the apostle *(far left)*

He is dressed as a pilgrim—his shrine at Santiago de Compostela in northern Spain was a very important pilgrimage centre in the Middle Ages, as it still is. He holds his pilgrim's staff, and at the bottom of his diagonal shoulder strap is part of a scallop shell, his symbol.

The archbishop St Denys *(right)*

This panel in white, gold and deep blue is exceptionally beautiful, and for this the 1966 restorers deserve great credit. The archbishop is saying Mass while in prison awaiting martyrdom. He has reached the climax at the Elevation of the Host. At this point the risen Christ surrounded by angels appears to him, completely obliterating any sign that this is in prison.

How do we know this is St Denys?

Legend has it that St Denys received this vision just before his death. Christ takes the newly-consecrated host (the bread for Holy Communion) from the archbishop's hand and gives it back to him saying 'Take this, my beloved'. The words from the legend, which was read in church annually at Matins on St Denys's day, are written on the scroll that Christ is holding. It goes on to say, above St Denys's head, 'Whoever you intercede for, your prayer will be granted.'

The indulgence—a unique survival

The three fragmentary lines of writing underneath St Denys are the only surviving 'indulgence' in any English medieval window.

An indulgence reduces or does away with the penalty

you have to pay for a sin once you have confessed it. You gain it by performing an important religious duty like undertaking a pilgrimage, or meditating on the mystery of the Mass, or invoking the prayers of our Lady and the saints.

This window features our Lady, and St James of Compostela pilgrimage fame, and St Denys who is saying Mass and the efficacy of whose prayers is moreover explicitly mentioned. The window thus fits an 'indulgence' theme very well, providing a possible solution to the mystery of why the window depicts these particular three main figures.

34 The Lady Chapel

This chapel, to the left (north) of the high Altar, was added to the church between 1200 and 1210. As the name implies, the chapel is dedicated to the mother of Jesus, the Blessed Virgin Mary, known 'our Lady'.

Amazing rediscovery of a statue

Soon after the Lady Chapel was built, a more-than-lifesize statue of our Lady was placed here, with a lamp permanently burning before it. Like many statues in churches it was entirely destroyed at the Reformation in the 16th century—or so everyone thought.

Amazingly, the head and shoulders of this statue were found again four centuries later, close to where it had originally stood.

Some shapeless lumps of stone in the surround of the Pricke of Conscience window were removed in the 1930s. They proved to be the head and shoulders of the old statue.

The face had been smashed— 'defaced'—but the wonderful carved hair survived, flowing down over her shoulders, hidden for four centuries.

This surviving piece is now in the floor-level niche to the right of the Altar in the Lady Chapel. The modern statue was carved to the same scale in 2012.

(below) The modern statue of our Lady

(below) The 'shapeless lumps' at the bottom right of a sketch made in 1908

(below) The surviving fragment of the medieval statue

A medieval spiritual insight

The Pricke of Conscience window, the statue and the Lady Altar together form a spiritual unit. The window calls people to a realisation of how fragile and finite human life is, faced with ecological, natural and spiritual disasters. They are invited to turn to Mary the mother of God and mother of the Church. She points to her Son, the Redeemer of the world, who is seen in the Sacrament of the Altar. This is a vivid little insight into medieval spirituality.

The 'paradise garden'

The lily

The monogram of 'Mary'

The floor tiles

The tile floor was installed in 2012. The tiles are hand-made in the medieval way – the pattern impressed into the damp clay and the impression filled with lighter-coloured clay known as 'slip'.

The patterns are copied from medieval tile fragments found in or near All Saints.

There are eleven circular roundels made up of 16 tiles each. In them fences enclose stags and lilies. Stags symbolise Christ, since popular belief held that stags could kill serpents. Lilies in their purity symbolise Mary.

Hence stags and lilies mean this is a 'paradise garden' with Christ and our Lady at play. Dogs are there also – are they symbols of faith ('fido')? Or are they hunting the stags, a sign that evil lurks even in paradise?

Oak-leaves outside the corners of each roundel root this scene in the familiar English landscape.

The angel ceiling

Made around 1470, the hammerbeam ceiling is adorned with twelve carved angels. They were originally brightly coloured, the effect of which can be seen in the adjacent Chancel ceiling (see p. 36) where the angels were repainted in the 1970s.

(far left) An angel holds a reliquary (a box for holding religious relics)

(left) An angel uses a plectrum to pluck a stringed instrument, probably a cithern

The Chancel

The Chancel, the central part of the church to the east of the Rood Screen, was built in two stages between 1100 and 1150. It contains the High Altar and other furnishings needed for the celebration of the Mass. The furnishings are all modern except for the spectacular Rector's Stall. The East Window was enlarged to its present size in 1330. The angel ceilings (see p. 38) date from c. 1470.

Image: Visiting North Yorkshire

(above) The Chancel

(left) The oak Stall of c. 1470. The two boards forming the back are more recent.

The Stall
The oak stall on the right-hand side of the chancel was made around 1470. The seat tips up, and on the underside it has a small ledge known as a 'misericord'. This was so that the priest could rest without sitting down, during long services when he was supposed to stay standing throughout. *Misericordia* means 'mercy' in Latin!

Because misericords were normally out of sight, they were often carved with amusing and even profane subjects, but this one is not. It has the initials IMG and coat of arms of John Gillyott, rector from 1469 to 1475, along with a carving of a mother pelican with her chicks.

The 'pious pelican' was a favourite symbol, for the mother pelican's habit of pecking at her breast while grooming gave rise to the legend that she was feeding her young with her own blood. Medieval piety linked this with Christ feeding us with his own blood in the Eucharist (or Mass).

(left) The misericord under the seat. The initials on the left read IMG, for John Gillyott, Rector 1469-1475, and his coat of arms is on the right. the centre the 'pious pelican' feeds her chicks on her own blood, as the legend had it, symbolising Christ feeding his flock with his blood in the Mass

The High Altar
Underneath the east window, this is the main altar in the church. Here the priest presides over the climax of the Mass, the offering of bread and wine to be given to worshippers in Holy Communion.

The coloured hangings
The front of the High Altar and of the Lectern are covered with hangings, the colour of which changes with the seasons. White is for the main festivals of Christmas and Easter and the weeks following. Purple is for the times of preparation for these, Advent and Lent. Green—the colour of life and growth—is for ordinary times. Red is for festivals of the Holy Spirit and of martyrs. Black is for Good Friday (the day of the crucifixion) and for funerals.

The screens

Intricately-carved oak screens fill the north, west and south sides of the Chancel. They were all made in the first quarter of the 20th century, imitating medieval models.

The screen on the west, separating the Chancel from the Nave, is the 'Rood Screen', so called because it carries the 'rood' or large crucifix which here reaches almost to the ceiling. On either side of the crucified Christ stand St Mary (on the north) and St John.

Beside the High Altar the screens separating the Chancel from the Lady Chapel (on the left) and the St Nicholas Chapel are virtuoso examples of 20th-century wood-carving of remarkable craftsmanship.

The Easter Sepulchre *(below, left)*

Set into the north wall to the left of the High Altar, this twin-arched recess is a very rare survival of an Easter Sepulchre.

On Good Friday (the day commemorating the crucifixion of Jesus), during worship a cross was held up for the people to venerate. (It still is.) In the Middle Ages this cross was taken at the end of the service to the Easter Sepulchre and 'buried' behind curtains. It was joyously retrieved on Easter Morning, a vivid symbol of the resurrection of Jesus.

The virtuoso carved oak screens to the north (foreground) and south (background) of the High Altar. The stone archways filled with these screens are irregular. They were created in 1210 on the north and 1340 on the south, when the two chapels were respectively built. The wood carver has skilfully adjusted his screens to fit the strange shapes of the arches.

(below) An elaborately carved thistle on the south screen

(below) The asymmetrical south arch and screen

Image: Visiting North Yorkshire

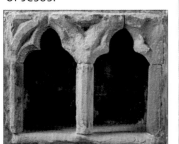

Image: Visiting North Yorkshire

The Rood Screen *(left)*

Every medieval church had a screen separating Nave from Chancel and carrying a 'rood', a representation of Christ on the cross. This screen was designed by Ridsdale Tate as a memorial to the Middleton family. Tate died in 1922, though the Rood Screen was not installed until 1926.

38 The Angel ceilings (1470)

15th-century angel ceilings spectacularly carved in oak cover the entire eastern half of the church. Those in the Chancel were painted in full colour in the 1970s. These colours give a good idea of the original appearance of all the ceilings—traces of the early paintwork survive here and there. The ceilings to left and right, over the Lady Chapel and the St Nicholas Chapel, have not yet been repainted.

The first angel on the north side of the Chancel, just inside the Rood Screen, carries in his left hand a model of All Saints complete with spire. He is signifying that the angels keep watch over the church.

The Annunciation

At the east end of the Chancel, above the High Altar, the last angel on the north is Gabriel (*above*) announcing to our Lady opposite (*right; she is the only ceiling figure without wings*) that she is to be the mother of God's Son.

(above) In the centre above the High Altar is the coat of arms of John Gillyott, rector of All Saints in the early 1470s, who had the angel ceilings made.

Angel musicians

Several musical angels assist at worship. They give a good indication of musical instruments of the 1470s.

A viol, played with a bow

A harpsichord—this is believed to be the earliest known representation in English art of any keyboard instrument. Strangely the instrument is in mirror-image, so that the longer bass strings are played by the right hand. The wood-carver can't have been a musician!

A portable organ: the right hand plays the keys, the left hand works the bellows. The single rank of pipes is in front of the angel, between his arms.

A cithern, plucked

Grotesques

Where the ceiling ribs meet, there are carved bosses in the form of grotesque figures.

Some of these are humorous - if we laugh at the Devil he flees.

Some have stylised animal heads.

There are several **'green men'**, faces with foliage growing out of their mouths and entwined around their heads.

The baptismal Font stands, as it always has done, just inside the entrance to the church. This is because Baptism is the rite of entry into the Church, the way you become a member.

The bowl of the Font is plain and unadorned and is of unknown date, though it is certainly medieval. It seems that the pillar it sits on is medieval too, but the base is modern.

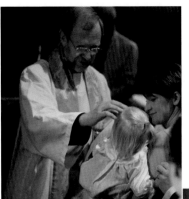

The person being baptised is sprinkled with water from the Font, marked with the sign of the Cross, and given a lighted candle.

These two images: John Cunningham

The Font cover (*right*)
The ornate tiered lid is mid-20th century in date, the work of the eminent church architect George Pace. It was designed to be raised and lowered by a pulley system, but this has been deemed unsafe. Instead the lid is now permanently fixed above the Font out of harm's way.

The sprinkling or immersion in the water of the Font is a symbolic sharing (by drowning and new birth) in the death of Christ on the cross and his resurrection from the dead. By this the person being baptised is made a member of the church and a sharer in the new life of Christ.

(right) The simple medieval Font on its modern base

Image: John and Merry Norman; John Hope Photography

The Bells

High up in the slender tower of 1394 is a ring of 8 bells used for change-ringing.

In the peculiarly English art of change-ringing each bell turns a complete 360° when rung, producing a very full and rich tone. Truly the ringers 'make a joyful noise unto the Lord'.

(above) Looking down on the bells

They are hung in a structure known as the bell frame. Each bell is attached to a large spoked wheel. The bell rope pulled by the ringer passes around the rim of this wheel.

(left) A red counterbalance weight on each bell makes rotating it easy.

The Organ

Music has always been vitally important in Christian worship. There was a saying in the Early Church that 'the one who sings prays twice'.

This mechanical-action instrument has two manuals and full pedal-board with 15 speaking stops. It was built in 1996-7 by Principal Pipe Organs of York, using parts from at least two previous organs.

Even in the medieval period All Saints was one of the city churches which possessed a pipe organ. And portable pipe organs are two of the instruments played by angel musicians on the chancel ceiling (p. 38) and the Lady Chapel ceiling.

Image: John and Merry Norman; John Hope Photography

42 Sculpture

Many statues and other carved objects were in All Saints in the Middle Ages and have now been lost or destroyed over the centuries. Nevertheless there are some notable survivals, as well as the fragment of the more-than-lifesize medieval statue of our Lady (p. 34), and the angel ceilings (p. 38). They include these:

(*left*) This very rare wooden statue, dating from around 1400, is one of a mere handful in the whole of England to survive the Reformation in the 16th century. It represents a bishop, probably St William of York (see p. 10-11).

It is not known where the statue was originally situated. It may not even have been made for All Saints at all.

(*right*) On the north side of the Chancel, the pillar nearest the Rood Screen is made of this large piece of Roman masonry. When the Lady Chapel was built around 1210 there must still have been bits of ancient Roman stonework lying around.

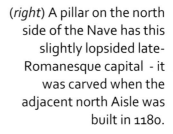

(*right*) A pillar on the north side of the Nave has this slightly lopsided late-Romanesque capital - it was carved when the adjacent north Aisle was built in 1180.

(*left*) A modern copy of the statue of St William stands on this corbel (carved stone bracket) at the north side of the Rood Screen facing the Nave.

The corbel is 14th-century but is carved in an archaic Romanesque style. The figure has unusually long sensitive fingers.

(*right*) Alabaster plaque of the early 15th century (not on display). It represents the Resurrection of Christ, with sleeping soldiers failing to guard the tomb. It is roughly contemporary with the anchorite Emma Raughton (see p. 44), and a local tradition has it that she used it as an aid to meditation.

Medieval stone grave markers

All Saints has 23 of these, the largest collection in York, more even than York Minster. They date from the 13th to the 15th century.

(*right*) This 15th-century slab, now partly obscured, is set in the floor of the St Nicholas Chapel. It marks the grave of Thomas of Yllingwyke and his wife Juliana.

Normally laid flat in the floor over graves, they were carved not usually with names but with symbols of those buried. Names begin to appear only towards the end of the medieval period, as in the illustration on the far right.

Most of them have been moved from their original positions, which are now unknown. Many are built into the walls, some of them outside - they were a useful source of dressed stone when the south wall was rebuilt in 1865.

They usually had a tall shaft with at the top a stylised cross, often in a circle. Beside the shaft can be found symbols of the person(s) buried.

(*left*) This splendid example is now standing upright against the inside of the west wall. It seems to have belonged to the grave of a married couple. On the right of the shaft is a sword (for the husband), and on the left a distaff (for the wife).

The change in colour shows a flood level! Before the flood protection wall was built opposite the church in the late 20th century, it was frequently inundated.

(*left*) A crudely carved chalice indicates the grave of a priest.

The two below are now set in the inside wall of the porch.

(*left*) What looks like a cleaver but may be a tanner's scraping tool could indicate the grave of a tanner, since Tanner Row is nearby.

(*right*) A sword and a bow and arrow presumably marked the grave of two comrades-in-arms.

44 The Anchorhold

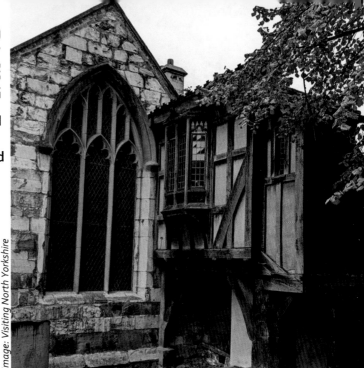

Image: Visiting North Yorkshire

All Saints, like several churches in medieval York, had an 'anchorhold'. This was a cell attached to the outside of the church where a solitary 'anchorite' lived a life devoted entirely to prayer and meditation. For food, drink and clothing he or she was completely dependent on gifts from parishioners. The word 'anchorite' means someone *withdrawn* from the world.

York's anchorholds were all destroyed at the Reformation. Uniquely, at the beginning of the 20th century the All Saints anchorhold was rebuilt.

It is outside the west (back) wall of the church. This is where the medieval Anchorhold was, as can be seen by the 'squint' through which the anchorite could take part at a distance in church services.

Emma Raughton
At All Saints the anchorites were women. The most famous of them was Emma Raughton, who lived in the Anchorhold for some years after 1420.

Emma's visions
During this time Emma received a series of seven visions of the Virgin Mary. In them our Lady told her that the upbringing of king Henry VI, then a small toddler, was to be entrusted to Richard Beauchamp, earl of Warwick. Our Lady also told Emma that Henry was to be crowned king in both England and France, despite being just a child.

Their outcome
Henry VI was indeed crowned in London, in 1429, Warwick holding him in his arms, and in Paris in 1431. The visions were written down some decades later. They are the best documented visions in the whole of medieval England.

(above) The Anchorhold outside the south Nave Aisle's west window

(near right) The Anchorhold is visible from inside that window. On the left is the squint looking down into church.

(far right) View from the Anchorhold through the squint into the south Aisle

Modern anchorites at All Saints
In the 20th century the Anchorhold has several times been home to a recluse. Most recently an anchorite, Brother Walter Willman, lived here for 30 years up to the early 1960s, becoming briefly famous after appearing on BBC TV's *Whicker's World* in 1961.

Archaeological Finds

All Saints with its churchyard has yielded many interesting finds. Here are some of them.

(above) Broken axe-head from the Iron Age (1200-600 BC)

Prehistoric York

The area was inhabited from prehistoric times, being at lowest (nearest the North Sea) easy crossing point of the river Ouse. The Iron-Age axe head is a recent find.

Roman York (Eboracum)

The Romans had a major fort and civil town here from the 1st to the 5th century. Several emperors had their summer residence in York, in a palace just up the hill from All Saints.

(above) Many pieces of Roman pottery have been found in the churchyard

The churchyard is full of fragments of Roman pottery, and interesting relics like these two tiny dice (*left; the Roman one at the far left is smaller than the medieval one also dug up in the churchyard*). A rare find was this beautiful Roman intaglio from a ring *(left)*.

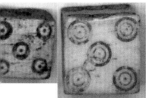

Anglian York

The 7th-8th century is York's 'Anglian period'—the Angles were the 'Anglo' part of the Anglo-Saxon invasions that followed the end of Roman rule in AD 410.

All Saints churchyard is the only place outside York's main Anglian settlement where rare Anglian

pottery has been found, including several pieces of antler-stamped pottery *(above)*. Each pattern has been carved in the exposed end of an antler after the tip has been cut off.

Anglo-Scandinavian York (Jorvik)

This is the 9th and 10th centuries, and is probably when All Saints was built. Among finds from this period is the beautifully carved spindle whorl, *right*.

Medieval joy and sadness

When the Lady Chapel was excavated in 2011-12 this magnificent set of four oyster shells was found *(right)* which had been used as paint dishes. Much of the original paint is still in them— red, blue, yellow; and flesh-colour mixed with mother-of-pearl. These will have been used for painting a statue, perhaps the great statue of our Lady (page 34).

A sad discovery under the Lady Chapel was a large double-chambered brick tomb, containing in one chamber the skeleton of a pregnant woman complete with her unborn full-term child.

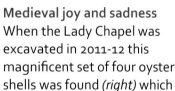

The evolution of the building

All Saints, like most medieval buildings, grew up over many centuries.

The first written mention of it that we know of is shortly after the Norman Conquest of 1066. But the church was already well established before the Conquest, occupying part of the present Nave.

The original pre-Conquest (Anglo-Saxon) church

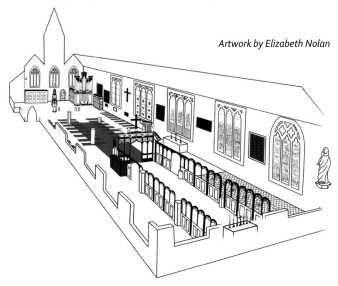

Artwork by Elizabeth Nolan

The original church was a simple rectangular building. It was the width of the present Nave minus side aisles but not as long, going from the pillars just east of the entrance door to those just east of the Rood Screen. Its floor occupied roughly the part of the floor coloured red in the sketch. It probably had a small semi-circular or rectangular chancel just inside the present Rood Screen.

Get your bearings

The conventional terms **'north'**, **'south'**, **'east'** **and 'west'** refer to parts of the church. The back of the church is at the west end, behind you if you are sitting in a pew. The High (main) Altar is at the east end. If you face it, the north side is on your left and south side on your right.

Halfway between east and west ends the Rood Screen divides the Nave (where most of the pews are) from the Chancel (where the High Altar is). On each side of the Nave and Chancel are side Aisles.

1066-1150: Norman enlargements

With the Normans came political stability and increased trading wealth, and the church was found to be too small. By 1150 a new Chancel had been built and then extended as far as the present East end. There were still no side aisles.

1180-1210: A major building programme

- The floor level was raised about 1m (3ft) to its existing level, probably because of flooding.
- The north wall of the Nave was pierced with arches and the north Nave Aisle was built, followed 10 years later by the south Aisle. (The 10-year gap is why opposite pillars in the Nave don't match.)
- Nave and Aisles were then extended westwards and the existing two north and south entrances made, replacing the former west door.
- The Lady Chapel was built 1200–1210, forming the north Chancel Aisle. (A Lady Chapel is so called because it is dedicated to St Mary, 'our Lady'.) Archways were made through the solid north wall of the Chancel to give access to it.

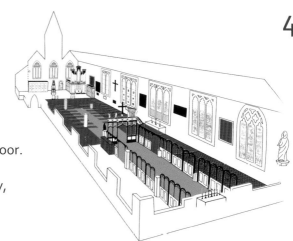

1340: the south Chancel Aisle

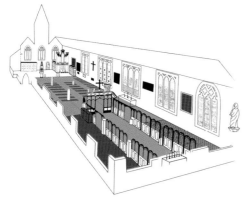

The south wall of the Chancel was pierced with arches and the south Chancel Aisle was built, forming the St Nicholas Chapel. In the late 19th century it was slightly widened to make it the same width as the south Nave Aisle.

1394: extension to the west

An entire new west wall was built, including the Anchorhold, and the slender octagonal tower and spire were added. As soon as it was finished, the half-timbered cottages that you see outside the Lady Chapel were built to house chantry priests. In 1394 a tanner, Richard Byrd, left 6/8 (£0.3) in his will 'To the new fabric of the church', this westward extension.

c. 1330: the first stained glass

The first stained glass windows to survive were installed in the East Window (later moved to the Lady Chapel) and the St Nicholas Chapel.

c.1420-c.1440: the rest of the stained glass

A tremendous burst of creativity at a time of growing trading prosperity in the parish led to the installation of the rest of the stained-glass windows.

48 The making of stained-glass windows

Glass in Britain, thanks to the Romans...
Glazing was introduced into Britain by the Romans in the first century AD and had became widespread by the third century.

...but not for long
When Roman rule collapsed in AD410 the art of making glass was lost.

Glass-making resumes in England
Glass making was reintroduced by the Saxon Church. Famously, Benedict Biscop, Abbot of Monkwearmouth in Co. Durham, sent to Gaul for glaziers in 675 'as there were none in England'. Glass-making furnaces dating to c. 690 have been found at Glastonbury Abbey.

(right) Painted image of Christ in an excavated window roundel, Ravenna, AD 540

Images on this page and the first image on p. 49: David Mercer

Why was glass wanted in churches?
The passage of light through the glass was seen as a symbol of the divine light of God, and the church developed glazing as a specifically Christian art form.

The first painted glass in churches
We do not know when windows were first painted. The oldest known example is from Ravenna, Italy, AD 540 (*above right*).

In England, the earliest painted glass is a fragment of glass found in excavations at Nunnminster, Winchester dating to the early 10th century.

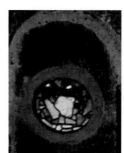

(above) Jarrow: Recreated Anglo-Saxon window

Development of the technology in England
Glass was made by melting sand. Adding wood ash was found to lower the temperature at which silica melts, so glass was made in densely wooded areas. By 1400 the Surrey-Sussex Weald had become the centre of the English Glass industry. Beech ash gave the glass a greenish hue.

Coloured glass was made by adding various chemicals to the molten glass. Thus adding cobalt produces a vivid blue.

This was technically difficult and in England Saxon churches used recycled Roman coloured material (*left*).

The zenith of English church glass-making
The 11th to the 15th centuries saw an explosion of creativity in English church glass.

By 1500 high-quality coloured glass could be found in even the smallest parish church in England. A whole industry sprang up to produce new windows, and by 1408 the new Great East Window of York Minster was the largest in Europe.

Wealthy individuals and corporations vied to commission new windows. In the York church of St Denys Walmgate a donor, Robert Skelton, is shown presenting his window (1350, *left*).

Making the glass into pictures
The sheets of different coloured glass were cut into small pieces and joined together by strips of lead, allowing the creation of elaborate pictures.

Line-art designs were painted on, to outline drapery etc. But each piece of glass was of uniform colour, as

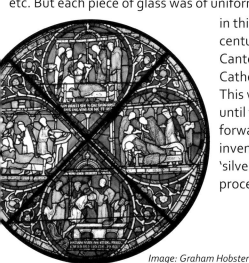

in this 13th-century panel in Canterbury Cathedral *(left)*. This was the case until the next step forward, the invention of the 'silver stain' process.

Image: Graham Hobster

Silver stain

Around 1300 a major technological breakthrough called the **silver stain process** enabled colour to be applied selectively to parts of a single piece of glass. This meant that for the first time a change of colour in the design did not require a new piece of glass and more lead edging. Glass treated like this is 'stained glass', as distinct from the 'painted glass' of the older technique.

The arrival of 'stained glass'
All the windows in All Saints are stained as well as painted. In this image of the Virgin Mary in the East Window (page 23) the heavy black line of lead shows clearly that her face, her hair, her nimbus (halo), her upper bodice and her hand are all on one single piece of white glass.

Painted black lines indicate her features and fingers. But the gold of her hair, nimbus and bodice are all 'stained' and would have been impossible without the technique.

The result was a marked increase in the delicacy of detail, as a comparison with the earlier Canterbury glass clearly shows.

We have come a long way from 670 when it was noted in amazement that bishop Wilfrid at York Minster 'by putting glass in the windows prevented the birds or the rain from getting in, without keeping out the rays of light.'